CW01573369

Treating the Untreatable is a collaborative writing project. The contributors are;

- Paradise Farr
- Ellie O'Mara
- Isabella Murray
- Alfie Spencer
- Christopher De Sa
- Iris Boddye-Kincaid
- Jeremy Ellis
- Leyester Aboagye-Barrow
- Isabella Gorden-Salem
- Amelia Hurst

with cover design from images by Kiyonobu Ito and cnicholsonpath', provided under a Creative Commons Licence. The project was overseen by Joe Reddington.

The group cheerfully acknowledges the wonderful help given by:

- Jennifer Allen
- Adam Messerli

And a big thank you goes to the SHINE Trust who funded this wonderful project. It's been a wonderful opportunity, and everyone involved has been filled with incredible knowledge and enthusiasm. Finally, we would like to thank all staff at John Roan for their support in releasing our novelists from lessons for a full week. The group started to plan out their novel at 9.15 on Monday 20 March 2017 and completed their last proof reading at 12.00 on Friday 26th March 2017. We are incredibly proud to state that every word of the story, every idea, every chapter and yes, every mistake, is entirely their own work. No teachers, parents or other students touched a single key during this process, and we would ask readers to keep this in mind. We are sure you will agree that this is an incredible achievement. It has been a true delight and privilege to see this group of young people turn into professional novelists in front of our very eyes.

Treating the Untreatable

Tim Cooks

White Water Writers

Chapter 1

The smell of smoke filled the air. Ashes fell from the cigarette onto the carpet as James Wood sat down in his chair, holding an envelope in his hand. There was an old antique clock situated by a large wooden table. Scattered across the table were pictures and pieces of paper from the last case that the detective James had worked on. A cabinet, with one draw missing, was filled with cigarette packets and the necessary tools for investigations. Streams of light peeked through the blinds and into the room. Dust floated through the air. The whole room seemed as though it hadn't be dusted or cleaned for a few a long time. The detective had dark brown hair and bluey-green eyes. He wore a hat and a long coat that reached down to his knees. The detective was tall and thin, but had small hands. James was a stubborn man who did not like other people's opinions and was independent as well as very untidy. Despite his ignorant nature, he was very caring, generous and extremely responsible. He took the cigarette out of his mouth, put it onto the old, broken ashtray and ripped the envelope open, tearing the letter in the process. He then pulled the letter out carefully, careful not to rip it any more than what it had been, he then unfolded it.

Dear James Wood, I am writing to tell you that I have a new case for you. Recently, there have been reports of strange sounds and noises around residential areas near Canary Wharf. I am asking you to solve this case because you are our most experienced and skilled detective. Please solve this case as soon as possible and report back to us when you have done so. Yours sincerely, Daniella M He then folded up the letter into a paper plane and threw it, watching it soar through the air until it gracefully landed on the floor. Apprehensively, the detective then stood up and rushed out the door. Hastily, the detective opened the door, forgetting to lock it and ran down the street. It was cold and damp outside. The trees swayed in the wind. The birds chirped in their nests and the squirrels ran up trees. Rusty railings separated the tall houses from the crowded roads. James needed to solve this case as soon as possible.

Chapter 2

Finally, Jayden arrived at Jackson's house after a long and tiring journey. The outside was a pretty beige colour, with a white door and white window frames. There was a silver knocker and a matching silver letter box outside, which was identical to all the other houses. Furthermore, there was a small front garden that contained a pathway, made of white pebbles, a flowerbed that surrounded the house, a batch of freshly mowed grass and a sprinkler (that was currently on, watering the grass and the flowers). There was a hedge surrounding the front garden. By the front door there were three bikes: one green, one blue, and one yellow. "Jayden, you're here. Finally!" "Hi Jackson." Jackson was wearing a long-sleeved light green top, a pair of dark blue trousers and some red converses. "Glad you could make it, come in." "Thanks for inviting me." Inside, Jackson's house was amazing, the walls were a bubbly milky white the hardwood floor was gleaming and the furniture looked like it had just been bought. The sofas were made from real black leather, with decorative gold studs. There was a 54 by 40 inch television screen with surround sound speakers that could be heard from anywhere in the house when at full volume. A heaven for any child and a peaceful studying area for when you needed to do your homework. Jayden was astonished as she started sorting out some familiar sheets of paper and began writing in a tattered and all-too -similar book-her homework book. “Come on, let’s have some fun. No boring homework yet.” “Ok Jackson, but we still need to do it.” “Jayden, we can do the homework after we have fun.” “Fine.” While having fun, Jackson and Jayden played ’Buckaroo’, ’Twister’, ’Would you Rather?’, and ’Never Have I Ever’. They also watched 5 episodes of Dennis the Menace and Gnasher with the surround sound on at full blast. The full scale of the television could finally be appreciated along with the surround sound. It was so loud, it made the floor tremble.

“Jackson, its quarter to five!” “So?” “Really, we need to get our homework done now or we will never do it!” “Okay, okay. We get this over and done with, and then I’ll get us something to eat.” “It’s a deal.” ”Jackson, do you know how to... wait, never mind.” ”What is it?” ”I was going to ask you how to factorise but I just remembered how to do it.” ”Do you think that Math is harder than they make it sound?” ”Sometimes.” “Jackson, where did you get these crisps? They are so good.” “The Co-operative.” Finally, they finished their homework. Afterwards, Jayden went home.

Chapter 3

The postman came through the creaky old gate and approached the blue varnished door. He picked up a pile of letters from his red bag and slotted them through the rusty letterbox. As he did this, Agnus came flying down the stairs at high speed, almost tripping on her night gown. She was expecting a letter, a very special letter. There it was, on the mat amongst the bills. She picked it up and slowly opened it. It recited: *Dear Agnus, We are delighted to inform you that you got the job as a doctor at Island Health. We hope to see you bright and early tomorrow morning and ready to go. Best Wishes, Ashton K And The Island Health Medical Team* Agnus jumped with joy at the thought of this. All her dreams had come true. Agnus was a 45 year old with a British accent. She had hazel eyes and rainbow-dyed hair. This went down to her shoulders. She was born on 31st of October. One thing that nobody knew about Agnus was that she had a mental health issue, but this does not stop her from getting ready. This was why Agnus wanted to be a doctor, to help people going through what she was. She had to take medication to help her cope with this. If she didn't, she had mood swings and became extremely dangerous. Her fear was people judging her for who she was. She had always wanted to be a doctor as a child and watched many medical TV programmes. As soon as she arrived at the hospital the next morning, she started to sweat with fright. She had waited for this moment all her life, she couldn't muck it up now. She slowly walked towards the desk that had a large sign over the top. It read "Reception". There was a man and lady at the desk that looked quite friendly and so Agnus didn't hesitate. When she got closer to the desk, the woman spoke, "How can I help you?" There was a long pause. Agnus didn't know what to say back at her. She didn't prepare for this. Eventually she answered back. "I am looking for the Neurosurgeon. I am the new recruit." As soon as these words came out of her mouth the lady and gentleman got distracted with another patient. They pointed in the direction of the office. Agnus left without saying a word. As she walked towards the office, she looked around so she could get her bearings. She made her way past the x-ray rooms and the supply rooms. The walls where bright orange and the seats were bright blue. It made her feel happy and safe. Even walking through the corridors she knew she was going to like it here. All the people were so nice. The hospital looked quite new as all the paint work was still intact and colourful. All the people looked happy and well looked after. Agnus was so happy. Once Agnus found the office, she entered. She was surprised to see the Neurosurgeon. All the other people in the hospital were so cheerful, but this man was not. He had a grey untidy beard and dark shallow eyes. Agnus was frightened. He spoke in a very old and wise way. "I heard you're new. So you're going to need a patient. Mrs. Wilkinson is in bay 2. I am sure you can handle that." After getting lost many times, she walked over to the bay very slowly, unsure what would be behind the curtain. Agnus pulled the curtain violently and saw a little old lady with a small cut down her leg. Apart from that meeting, Agnus' day was good. She had a fulfilling day helping people. She walked out, past the entrance. She felt like she was on a cloud and couldn't wait to go back in the morning. She hopped on the bus but didn't have enough on her Oyster card. The driver let her on anyway. As she got off the bus, she got soaked from the pouring rain. Fortunately for her, she lived around the corner so she could get changed and dried quickly. As she opened her old wooden gate, she dropped her keys in a muddy puddle. "Great! That's all I need!" She bent down and picked them up right as a car came past... straight through the puddle. She picked them up and got in the front door. The first thing she did was collapse on the sofa. Agnus' house was very old fashioned. She had twenty-five year-old floral wallpaper that had started peeling off the walls. She also had a desk with one leg missing, a fridge with a broken light, no electricity and barely any food. She liked to live that way. Her house was in a small road in the middle of Island Gardens. It was a row of around twenty houses all joined onto each other. Each of the houses were identical on the inside as they were on the outside. They all had one bedroom, one bathroom, one kitchen, one storage room and a small six foot by three foot garden. Even though it was tiny, it was large enough for Agnus. She only shared it with her black and white cat called Cookie. She had always lived alone as far back as she could remember. Another thing that most people didn't notice about the houses from the outside was that they have a downstairs which was originally the storage are, however Agnus didn't have many possessions. That night, Agnus decided to have her favourite dinner-pizza with potato and tuna toppings. She grabbed a tin of tuna and put it on the counter. She then got the potatoes from the slanted cupboard. Lastly, she got the pizza base from the broken fridge, poured the tin of tuna onto the pizza base, chopped up the potatoes and put them on. Finally she put everything into the oven. After about half an hour, Agnus got the pizza out of the oven and took it to her old sofa. She didn't have a television to watch so she just sat there in silence. Cookie came and sat on her lap and started to purr.

Chapter 4

A giant skyscraper stood ominously in the heart of Canary Wharf. There were rumours of this very tower of people disappearing upon entering. One you entered, you were greeted with smiling scientists and doctors. However, as people headed further through the building, they noticed that the tea and coffee were the only thing to look forward to. The whole tower was like a little girl had designed the place, if the little girl was obsessed with murder. “I feel like I’m getting cuter as I speak.” A little girl said brushing her golden hair. Her name was Lady Bella Tron. Her parents had suffered from a serious form of cancer in its third stage. Since her parents died, everything had been the same for lord master Bella Tron. She was planning to build a time machine along with the formula to cure her parent’s cancer. Her plan was to go back in time to cure her parents from brain cancer and be loved again. ”Soon mother and father you shall live again and love me, ” she said, staring at a portrait of her parents. ”Butler, ” she screamed. The butler entered nervously, ”Yes Mistress?” She said, ”Make me a hamburger!” ”Yes mistress.”

Chapter 5

As Jackson pulled his tie around his neck and began tying it, he was half way out of the door. "Bye mum!" Jackson yelled. The fresh air filled Jackson's lungs as he was met with a refreshing, soft breeze when he stepped outside. He could hear the birds singing their morning song When Jackson reached the corner by the train station, he was met by Jayden, who was wearing her school uniform which consisted of: a dark blue blazer and tie which both had the school crest on them, a black skirt, black shoes, and a long-sleeved white shirt. “Hey, Jayden, are you catching the train today?” Jackson asked. “No, I’m just going to walk for five hours and completely avoid all other forms of transport, ”Jayden replied sarcastically. Roughly ten minutes had passed since Jackson and Jayden entered the train station, when the train came speeding on the tracks until it came to a sudden halt when it reached the station, and the two friends boarded onto it. “I’ve got French upstairs first period, what about you?” said Jackson as he gazed at a classroom on the second floor of his school. ”English with Mr Reece, ”Jayden replied. The school had two floors, pale white walls, and grass, trees and benches surrounding it, the only exception being the path to the front entrance. Jackson and Jayden entered the school and parted ways and went to their separate lessons. Just over five hours later, Jackson and Jayden were in their Maths lesson with long faces. It was the largest room in the entire building, after the lunch hall and the assembly hall. Jackson sat on the front row, next to the most colourful wall in the room seat in front of Jayden. They were doing algebra, something Jackson could never understand. "Hey Jayden, how do you do question six?" Jackson whispered. "What?" Jayden whispered back. "What is the answer to question six?" "Question six? Err, I think it's two." "You don't seem sure about it." "I am sure!" "Alright, alright, "Jackson answered, turning around to write down the information he acquired. The lesson ended twenty minutes later. Once at home, Jackson collapsed on the sofa. He was exhausted after the long day at school. He hated Mondays. His first period of the day was French. His teacher, Miss Fanse, barely understood anything in English. Afterwards, it was history and then double science. Jackson would get at least one detention every science lesson by his teacher Mr Northwest. The final lesson was Geography. He barely understood any questions that he was asked to answer-especially ones to do with global warming. Once he had eaten his lasagne, he put on his headphones, turned on music to full volume and headed up to his bedroom. He turned off his bedroom light and then wrapped himself in the bedcovers while thinking about his mother. About an hour later, his mum walked through the doorway. "Good night, " his mum said as she kissed him on the cheek. "Good night, " Jackson whispered. "Love you." She closed the door. After listening to his music. He started to read, but half an hour later he started to feel sleepy, so he took of his headphones, closed his book and went to sleep.

Chapter 6

Zo Johnson was a counsellor for many people. She was five foot nine with hazel eyes and shoulder length, curly, brown hair. She wanted to help other people it was the thing she wanted to do the most, her life goal. Her favourite foods were pepperoni pizza and chicken and chips and she also liked to listen to pop music, especially Beyonc. Her favourite colours were admiral blue and gold. Although she wanted to help others, Zo was terrified of death, as well as not being able to counsel someone properly. Zo Smith (Smith being her maiden name) was born on Sunday the 20th of July 1980 in West London. As a child, she did exceptionally well at school, receiving almost straight A's and A* in her GCSE results, with the exception of one B in English Literature. She then went to University College London and studied psychology for five years. She met her late husband, Anthony, there and they married two years after the course finished. They didn't have any children, and Anthony died when Zo was 30. After that, the widowed Zo became a mentor and a counsellor. Zo was in her home on Manilla Street, fretting, stressing and just generally worried about her appointment. She had booked an appointment at Island Health to have a check-up, but she believed that she could have MS - the other people who wanted to "help" her with her health would not arrange for anything to help Zo without an official diagnosis, not just "I searched it up and all of my symptoms are those of MS." Zo thought that her new GP might not believe her, and that she would have to go through the whole palaver of getting referred and waiting for over three months to make an appointment, then wait for three weeks for the letter with the appointment time, then reschedule the appointment, and wait for the appointment. On the 277 to Cross harb, there was the usual hustle and bustle during the rush hour. So much so, in fact, that Zo couldn't hear herself think. She was trying to think about what the GP would say- whether she would listen patiently and then refer her, or if she would diagnose Zo with MS straight away. She got off the bus with a sinking feeling in her stomach. She didn't want to get off the bus but she knew she had to. The pathway towards the entrance had never felt so long like this. It felt like hours, with each step taking ten minutes. As she went through the doors of the hospital, she started to shake violently with fear. Zo approached the desk with small steps, she wanted the day to end. The receptionist told her to go to the waiting area and sit there until she was called. She entered the spacious, fanned waiting area she thought she was going to pass out. There was only a little old lady in there so she took the seat nearest to the door. Her thoughts where racing. What would she do if she did have M.S? How would she cope? So many questions with no answers to them. After around 20 minutes of sitting in absolute silence, the little old lady spoke. "Are you OK my dear? You look so pale." Zo, of course, hadn't noticed, but her face had gone as white as a sheet of paper. "I'm fine thank you. Just a little flustered." As soon as she said this, the old lady looked at her in a weird way and she felt very anxious now. "Why don't I get you a cup of tea?" Zo agreed and the lady was gone for approximately 3 minutes when Zo's name was called. A lady was standing waiting at the door when Zo approached. She looked very caring and Zo knew she could talk to her about anything. The first thing Zo saw when they entered the room was a really bright fish tank with two tropical fish. They were soothing in a way, and she didn't feel so bad anymore. She sat down in a very comfortable white chair. "What symptoms have you been having?" the doctor asked in a soft, calm voice. Zo explained what was going on and had a few tests done. At roughly 4:20pm the doctor came back and sat down silently. She had a serious look on her face. Zo knew that it couldn't be good news. She was correct. "You have M.S. There are many ways we can help support you but it doesn't look like you want to talk about that right now. Go home and have a rest. We will call you." Zo slowly backed out of the room and towards the bus stop. She somehow made it to the bus stop. The world seemed to be spinning around her and everything suddenly went dark. When she woke up she was on the floor. She had only blacked out for a few seconds, but there was a crowd of people around her. "What can I do to help "They were all saying, but Zo just shook her head and said thank you. She didn't need anyone else's help as long as she could get to the bus stop. When the bus came, her head was still spinning. She couldn't have M.S. It must have been a mix up. Her thoughts where still not settled when she headed to bed that night. The next week was like any other. She got a call from her agency about another patient she needs to council. The only difference about this was that it was a doctor from the hospital where she was diagnosed. That made Zo feel a little bit better as she now knew that even people who help other people sometimes need help themselves. When that day came Zo felt excited. She had no reason to, she just did. At dead on 3pm the short doctor walked through the door of the counselling room. It was the same doctor that had diagnosed her. Agnes. She didn't say anything, she just came in and sat down. She looked a little bit embarrassed to be there. "Don't worry. No-one is going to judge you here. You can tell me everything." The next 20 minutes where spent with the doctor opening about her problem. They both sorted out when they would meet again and where they would talk. When Agnes got home from the counselling meeting with Zo, she felt like there was more she could do to help. So she went to the local library and spent the next four hours on varied websites; including the NHS website and Wikipedia. She eventually got home at nine pm and put all of her research together. She didn't fall asleep until twelve am and still didn't think she had enough information. She really wanted to make it better and easier for Zo now that she was helping her.

Chapter 7

The scared scientist walked towards the large stone castle. A chill ran down his spine. The scientist gulped. He was mortified. The dark castle shadowed over the small scientist as he walked up to the door. He held his breath as he knocked. For a few moments, there was nothing but silence; he was alone outside. Then he heard footsteps from behind the castle doors. The doors opened. It was just a butler. The butler had a very smart black tuxedo on and a beard. “Ah, you must be the scientist that mistress has been talking about, ” he said, ”Come in, come in, she’s upstairs but be careful, she’s not in a very good mood today as she’s missed her morning nap.” Tom was a little confused by “morning nap”. He started to question what age Bella Tron actually was. Every time Tom remembered where he was, he felt fear rush through his body. He didn’t know what she wanted. All he knew was that she was a mighty woman named Bella Tron. The scientist was confused worried and scared, scared that this castle was so big he just knew he might get lost, he could feel it. The man slowly walked along the vast hall way, shivering with every step and every creak. He was now sweating with fear,

fear of the castle, terror of the all mighty Bella Tron and her powerful scientist empire. Tom was petrified. He knocked the door loudly and it echoed through the corridor. There was a pause. "Enter" exclaimed the almighty Bella Tron. Tom entered and was baffled to find a small girl who looked about four years old. "What are you staring at?" She snapped. "Err... um... I thought you would be older" said the scientist, surprised. "Older... you don't need to be old to rule the world one day! " she said. "Ah, yes you're obviously old and wise" he responded. "Hm. I have heard that you are an extremely smart and intelligent scientist. I believe that you could do something for me. So, what I want you to do, is find a cure for cancer, then, build a time machine, okay?" she explained. The scientist was in shock. "Err... well... that... that could take y-" "I will give you all the necessary materials to make this time machine and this cure for brain cancer. Every scientist in my lab will help you, " Bella Tron's voice deepened as this was. It seemed as though it could freeze the most villainous of criminals at an instant. Her deep voice trailed off into a soft, more comforting voice. A voice that you would hear if an adult was speaking to a small, young child. "In return I will pay you handsomely" "How much money?" Demanded Professor Edison. "Five-hundred thousand pounds, but, remember, you only have a short amount of time. Let's say... two weeks." "B-but-but I ca-" "Leave me!" she screamed. This made the butler appear in an instant, pulling the scientist out of the room and into the corridor. Bella Tron sat on her chair, thinking about what happened a few years back. 'I have to do this, I have to for my parents. No-one will stand in my way. I'll get what I want!' The butler escorted the scientist to the front door and bowed as a gesture of appreciation. He then closed the door, leaving the scientist to his own thoughts and leaving the scientist to wonder why Bella Tron needed a time machine and cure for cancer.

Chapter 8

As Jackson crept up the stairs, all he could think about was how strange his mum had been acting lately. Sometimes she would just look at me and cry, ' Jackson thought. Once he was in front of his mum's room, Jackson reached out to the silver door handle and pulled the door, which creaked as it opened. All the velvet curtains were closed, so the only light was that which was provided by a small lamp. The walls were a creamy white. The wooden floorboards were glossy and looked brand new, the king sized bed in the centre of the room was covered in blue and white pillows and blankets. The bedside tables matched the floor. Jackson slowly walked towards the old, creaky bed and sat next to his mother. He could feel tears desperately trying to roll down his cheeks, but he held them back as he knew it would only make his mum cry even more. "J-Jackson I h-have to t-tell you that I h-have c-can-" Jackson's mum said, before crying even more. "What? What do you have?" Jackson asked, the tears starting to overwhelm him. "C-cancer." Jackson was left speechless while tears flowed endlessly down his face. Jackson got up and left, leaving the door open behind him. He dragged himself sluggishly to his room, thoughts about his mum dying flooding his mind. Why did it have to happen to my mum? Why?' Jackson thought. Upon entering his room, Jackson let himself fall onto his bed and stayed there for several hours, until he eventually fell asleep. Jackson was in a room that was completely alien to him, there were strange devices everywhere, some of them broken and some of them working. Directly in front of him there was a book open on a page with a title of 'How to cure cancer'. Jackson reached out to grab it, when he felt a strange substance flowing through his veins, and death tighten its grasp around him. It burned like the fires of hell, and it made his heart hurt. Jackson felt his knees tremble as they collided with the floor and the rest of his body followed. His body was as cold as ice at this point and his vision was getting blurry. Everything went black Jackson woke up.

Chapter 9

"Hey Tom, can I ask you a favour please?" Shannon asked putting the phone to her ear. "Hey Shannon, yeah sure, what's up? Tom said. "I have to go shopping today and I was wondering if you would look after Izzy for me, Jackson is going to his friend's house so he can't look after her" Shannon said pleadingly. "Of course, just bring her to my house when you're ready" Tom said kindly. "Thank you so much!

You're a life saver. I will be round shortly. Bye, " Shannon said with gratitude. They both but the phone down an Shannon shouted, "Izzy, get ready Tom is going to babysit you while I go shopping" "Okay, I will be 10 minutes, " Izzy yelled back. Izzy and Shannon arrived at Tom's house one hour later. The front door was an orange, beige colour and had a diamond shaped doorbell which made a bird noise when it was pressed. The inside of the house was filled with fun and extravagant things. The walls were freshly painted and a strip of wall paper. There were chandeliers hanging from each end of the ceiling and the floor was dotted with tiles with a green and pink pattern. The kitchen had a blue fridge and a multicolour pack of cutlery hanging by magnets on the walls. The microwave was florescent yellow and the glasses were red, orange and purple. Tom had brown hair and brown eyes. He had an odd fashion sense. He wore a long sleeved t-shirt and orange jeans that flared down at the end. He had a hard to understand personality. He was happy one minute and then sad the next but he was a really nice person who you could tell anything to, no matter how important or unimportant it was. "Hey Izzy, do you want to take a look around, " Tom said to Izzy, "I am going to do some work so feel free." "Ok, thanks, " Izzy mumbled while typing on her phone. Izzy got up and started to look around. She went up the red carpeted stairs to a hall way. She saw three rooms. Izzy entered the first one which seemed like a spare bedroom. Izzy decided to leave that room and just go back down stairs. Two hours went by and it came up to lunch time and Izzy was getting hungry. Tom asked, "Izzy would you like some lunch? I am about to make myself a sandwich if you would like one" "Yes please, can I have ham?" Izzy politely asked while looking away from the television screen. "Ok, it should only be a few minutes" Tom said walking into the kitchen. Tom brought out a sandwich on a green plate to Izzy with a glass of apple juice "Thank you" Izzy said taking a sip from her apple juice. Izzy ate her sandwich and continued watching television. "Hey Tom, so how do you know my mum anyway?" Izzy said sitting on the orange sofa next to him "Well, your mum and I went to university together, we met when we had a free lesson together. We both liked eachother so we started talking and became really good friends." "Oh, okay, cool, " Izzy said while not even listening.

Chapter 10

Izzy was still at Tom's house. She was just sitting on the comfortable, orange sofa while Tom did some work. She was just thinking about her mum, who had been acting really strange lately. She had been weak, lifeless and just not her usual self. It was really starting to worry Izzy, as she had never seen her mum like this, she was normally fun, joyful and upbeat. Izzy started to wonder if Jackson had noticed it too.

Izzy decided to call Jackson and ask him. He was at his friend's house but this was way more important it was about their mum. She picked up her phone and dialled Jackson's number. It rang but went to voicemail. Izzy called again and again and again and finally (on the 5th try) Jackson answered. "Hello?!" Jackson asked, "What's wrong?" "Nothing, I wanted to talk to you about mum, she has been acting really strange lately. Have you noticed it?" Izzy murmured worryingly. "Izzy, look there is nothing to worry about. I'm sure mum is fine, she is probably just a bit sick or something. There is nothing to worry about, " Jackson said guiltily. "Are you sure?" Izzy questioned. "Yes, Izzy. Calm down everything is fine, I have to go ok? I will talk to you when we get home. Bye!"

A little bit later on in the day, Izzy still couldn't get her mum out of her mind. Jackson said not to worry but that was exactly what she was doing. Izzy was just worried about her mum and she wanted to help, but no one would tell her anything all they said was that she was fine. Not even her mum would tell her what was wrong! She texted Jackson, "Hey, are you sure there is nothing wrong with mum?" Izzy sat there waiting anxiously for her phone to buzz, a few minutes of torture her phone finally vibrated. "Izzy, you need to calm down. Nothing is wrong with mum, I know you're worried but you need to chill out." Izzy decided that enough was enough. She called her mum to ask what was going on, but she did not know her mum was not out shopping. It rang but did not answer.

This just made Izzy more worried about her. First her mum was acting strange, and now she wouldn't answer her phone! What was going on here? Izzy was so worried. She wanted to help her mum but she didn't know how. Izzy had an idea. She asked Tom if he knew what was going on. "Tom, can I ask you something?" Izzy asked. Tom looked up from his laptop screen, "Oh, um, yeah, sure Izzy. What is it?" "Well, it's my mum, she has been acting really strange lately, she is usually so fun and energetic but now she is weak and exhausted, she is just not the same." Izzy murmured. "Izzy, listen. I'm sure your mum is fine. If something was wrong I'm sure she would tell you." Tom said considerately and worriedly.

Chapter 11

Tom headed down to the laboratory and started to work on his time machine. A few minutes later Tom received an email from Bella Tron. Unfortunately hid computer was upstairs in his bed room. In his haste, he left the door to the laboratory open by mistake. Izzy, with great curiosity, went into the lab. Meanwhile, the scientist read through his email and responded to it. Suddenly, he heard a noise coming from the lab. Izzy had accidently broken the time machine! Tom ran down to the lab. "What have you done?" "Oh, I just pressed a few buttons..." "Do you have any idea what this means?" "Of course I don't!" Tom pushed Izzy out of the door hurriedly. Apprehensively, he decided to email Bella Tron. *Dear lord mighty Bella Tron, I would like to inform you that the cure for cancer is completely finished. But, the time machine has been destroyed by a thirteen-year old girl. I am sorry for this inconvenience, and would like to know if I could have another week to repair it. I will not let you down if you give me this opportunity. Yours Loyally, Thomas Edison* He got really angry at Izzy and lashed out. He takes one look at his time machine and realizes what she has done. Tom knows what she has done and he knows that Master Bella Tron will be so mad. He thinks of moving out of the country but then he needs the money to go. He realizes that it won't work and that he will have to go on the other side of the world if he doesn't want her to find him. "Oh well, I need to think of a plan to fix this before she sees it. IM IN SO MUCH TROUBLE! You don't even know what you have done to my life and now thanks to you it's over, " yelled Tom to Izzy. He threw her out the door and left her to perish.

Chapter 12

As Shannon walked out of the door, she swivelled round to kiss goodbye to Jackson. He wished her a good time shopping. She strolled out the door, unlocked her car and got in. The beautiful, glistening, red car shone in the sun as she steered down the road. Shannon drove further down the road and found the entrance to Island Health Hospital. She parked the car, got out and locked it so no one could take it. Shannon walked up to the door of the grand hospital and hoped she would be okay. She walked up to the counter and asked what would happen. The member of staff was unable to help her as he was just a receptionist. She checked in and went to sit down. Shannon was wondering what they would do to her. The yellow and grey doors opened again as Agnes walked through. She shouted, "Ms Shannon Edwards, please make your way to room 64-B." She walked down the corridor with the nurse. The nurse opened the door for Shannon to enter. She laid down on the bed while Agnes checked her documents on her computers. Shannon asked the nurse what would be done. "All we are going to do is take some blood tests and a urine test, " said Agnes with a soft voice. Her rainbow hair and hazel eyes made her feel more comfortable. Agnes reassured Shannon that everything was going to be fine. "This might make you feel a bit woozy, but you will be fine, " Agnes said as she inserted the needle into her elbow pit. She pulled the trigger and the blood rushed into the needle as if it was a crowd of people rushing into a store with a sale. The nurse asked her how she felt. "I feel light headed and I hope they come back negative." Agnes walked out of the room and she went to the office where the results were printing. She looked at them as she strolled down the corridor while heading back to room 64-B, where Shannon waited nervously. Agnes looked on the end page and her results were positive. As she wandered further towards the room, the guilt on her face became clearer as she got closer. Agnes sat down and put the sheets of paper down on the table facing down so she couldn't see them. Shannon sat up. "I'm really sorry to have to tell you this, but you have brain cancer and if we don't treat it, it could threaten your life, " announced Agnes in a sorry tone. Shannon asked her what treatment could be done to get rid of the cancer before it got worse. Agnes said that the only treatment would be chemotherapy. Shannon asked about check-ups and other appointments. She opened the door, her hands were shaking like an electric back massager. She walked up to her car and unlocked it. Once at home, Jackson asked how shopping was. "I didn't go shopping, I went to Island Health." "Why?" Jackson asked very concerned. "I was diagnosed with brain cancer. I didn't want to tell you or Izzy because I didn't want you to worry and Izzy's so young still. Promise me that you won't tell her." She explained, getting upset. "I promise."

Chapter 13

It was freezing outside. The sky was grey and miserable. The streets were quiet, quieter than they had been for the past few days. Jackson was strolling towards the library. He had to find out how he could prevent his mother's cancer from reaching a severe state where it could not be cured. He wished he could find some information for a cancer cure. The library had shelves full of books, which gave Jackson hope of finding even a little bit of a clue to a formula or something to help get rid of cancer. He hoped and hoped but he wasn't really believing in himself. Jackson went through piles of books about organs, cancer and doctors. His hope was rapidly fading away as the stack of unread books shrunk. Hours and hours passed and still he found nothing. The hope of helping his mum eventually faded and disappeared. Jackson flung his blue rucksack over his shoulder and left the library with his chin to his chest and his spirits low. He gave up on his wishes and made his way home in the gloomy rain. He arrived home soaked, tired and disheartened. He felt stupid trying to find something as not even the greatest scientists could find a cure. He felt like a failure, a complete and utter failure. He was ashamed. “I should have never gone to the library, ” Jackson mumbled to himself as he threw himself onto his bed.

Chapter 14

After returning from the library, his mum, Shannon, tried to calm him down but it was no use. He stormed out of the house. His vision was blurry, tears were rolling down his face from his green eyes. He didn't care where he was going or what he was going to do, but what he did know was that he needed to get away from home and that he would not come back for a few hours. He ran far away, so far away that he didn't know where he was. After an hour, Jackson's stomach started to rumble, as it had been several hours since he had eaten something. He hadn't eaten all day because he was worried about his mother. He was starting to feel homesick. He tried to make his way back home but he couldn't. Eventually, he gave up and asked a person walking passed for some help. "Hi, um, sorry could you please help me?" Asked Jackson slightly embarrassed "Yes, of course dear." "Thank you. I need to get to Canary Wharf from to be honest, I don't really know where we are, " Jackson said sheepishly "Oh, don't worry, we are in Island Gardens. Canary Wharf is about half a half an hour's walk away, how did you get here?" "Could you please tell me how I can get back to Canary Wharf?!" Jackson said raising his voice "Oh yes, sorry, I'll drive you there. It will take us about ten minutes, if the traffic is good." "Thank you. Could you please drop me off at Byng Street?" As he opened the door he took out his phone and dialled the number his mum gave him for counselling sessions. Jackson arrived at home within ten minutes, just like the stranger said they would. "I never did get her name" Jackson said thinking out loud, walking towards the door. "Who's name dear?" said Shannon opening the front door, relieved to see Jackson. "Don't worry mum." "Oh, okay, " Shannon's eyes and her nose was red - she was crying because she was worried. She had tears rolling down her big, red, hill-like cheeks. She had been crying a lot because of how Jackson reacted. He went upstairs to his room and he dialled the number for counselling again. It rang for a while and then someone picked up. "Hello, Canary Wharf Therapy. How may I help?" "Hi, my name is Jackson Edwards and I would like to book an appointment, " "Okay, my name is Zo and I am here to help you and take you through the steps of counselling. Is that okay?" "Yes, that's fine, " "All right, let's get started. First of all I need your date of birth" "That would be the third of September 2001." "All right..." The conversation continued as Zo asked more questions and Jackson answered them. But, near the end of the conversation, Jackson started to breath unevenly. "Yes, " responded Jackson in a shaky voice. "Are you sure?" "Yes, yes, yes, yes, yes everything is A-Okay" Jackson laughed uncertainly and nervously. "Are you sure?" "Yes!" screamed Jackson. "Remember, the deadline for you to get back to me about your counselling session is tomorrow, five pm sharp." "She's really annoying" thought Jackson. "How about this for a deadline!" Jackson said as he hung up the phone He thought back to what had happened that day; his eyes filled with tears as he remembered the time earlier on that day when he was told the terrible news. He started to sob as his mum entered the room. His mum comforted him. Izzy came into his room and said, "Hello you said we could play Minecraft on the Xbox 360. Come on- let's go!" She dragged him out of the room and down the stairs, sat herself down and patted the seat next to her, gesturing for Jackson to sit down. The rest of the day was fine and Jackson soon forgot about his dilemmas.

Chapter 15

Jayden was on the train heading towards Canary Wharf, where Jackson lived. "I wonder why he wants me to come to his house so late at night, maybe just to do homework..." Jayden thought as she stared out of the window. Once she arrived at Jackson's house, Jayden knocked on the door seven times, a sign that it was her at the door. The door swung open, and Jackson stood there with a worried expression on his face. "Why did you call me to do homework at six in the evening?" Jayden said, sounding slightly irritated. "That's not important, just come inside, " Jackson responded. Inside, Jackson and Jayden talked about school and homework, until Izzy burst into the room. "Izzy, what are you doing here? Aren't you supposed to be at Tom's house?" exclaimed Jackson. "I came here to tell you that Tom is secretly a scientist, and he has a lab under his house, where he is building a time machine and" "THAT'S NONSENSE!!" exclaimed Jackson "Now's not the time to be playing stupid kids' games. Anyway, you're too old. Now leave me alone!" "Just follow me." Jackson begrudgingly followed Izzy - just to try and prove a point. They both made their way to Tom's house along with Jayden. They arrive at Tom's house roughly five minutes after they left. They all stopped at the gate to try and decide how they were going to get in. "There's a gate around the side. That's how I got out. It's quite tight but I am sure you'll fit." "Come on! This is trespassing!" Jackson moaned wanting to go home. Reluctantly they all travelled into the back garden through the little hole in the brick wall. They headed towards the back door and it was open. They all snuck in (Izzy went first) and headed down the stairs towards the basement. As soon as they got to the top of the stairs Jackson apologised for his mistake. Right before him was Tom in a white lab coat standing in front of a large metal tin-shaped thing. "What is he making?" Jayden asked very curiously.

“The cure for cancer. This is going to save Mum. Jackson, you have to get it. No matter what you do!” They had a look around the house to see if there was anything they could use to help. They headed home as they needed to think of a plan

Chapter 16

Bella Tron had just reviewed her security and caught a boy roaming around. She was furious and had a temper tantrum. She was not happy so she phoned up the scientist and told him to poison the boy. “I’m sorry, Lord Master, I can’t poison him you don’t know what his mum’s going through!” “I don’t care! Poison the boy or I will poison you! In fact, poison him and his family, OK?” “Ok fine, I will poison him but I won't be happy if I have to go to prison when you should." "Prison-schmison I don't care, just do it!" Bella Tron hung up the phone because she was sick and tired of his backchatting. Tom was so scared, he didn't know what to do, so he baked some cookies with a secret ingredient in it and went to Shannon's house to give them to her. "Now Shannon, these cookies aren't for you. OK? They're for your son, Jackson, as he helped me out with his sister" lied Tom. "OK, sure. I'm on a diet anyway. Thanks a lot Tom, that's very sweet. Bye now!" "Bye!" The trap was set and it was going well so far. They were all falling for it. A couple of hours later, Shannon heard Jackson arrive home from school. "Hi Mum, I'm home!" yelled Jackson with an exhausted voice. "Ok son,

I have some biscuits for you and I have put them in your room. Tom came round and gave them to you because of you helping out with Izzy. I knew you were a good boy." "Yum, I am hungry!" said Jackson while rubbing his stomach with hunger. He ate a cookie that was sitting on the side. He was a bit cautious but they looked nice anyway.

Chapter 17

Jackson and Jayden headed back to Tom's house. They stole the cure for cancer and they had nearly made it back to the stairs again when suddenly, Jayden watched Jackson's body fall to the ground. It was limp. It was dead. The scientist was cackling and dancing before scurrying back to his desk to do something on his computer. Jayden was extremely upset, and started crying. She wanted to scream out loud but she knew better screaming would only make the situation worse. She had two options: Option One was to run out before the scientist caught her; Option Two was to keep hiding till the scientist left. She went with Option One. Jayden ran faster than she had ever done before, through the industrial hallway and out the other end. She was halfway through the entrance hall when Jayden decided to stop running and take a breath. Her eardrums rang with an ear splitting shriek the scientist was screaming: "WHAT??!! A GIRL WAS IN HERE WITH THAT BOY??!! NOOOOOO!!!!! NO-ONE OUTSMARTS TOM EDISON!" "Run Jayden, run!" Jayden thought to herself, and with a last sprint she made it through the entrance. Jayden felt the cold air hit her face and she knew that she was out of the evil lair. She was processing all the information when she realized that it would be better to do it on the way home, so she called her mum and asked her if she could be picked up. While in the car, Jayden could not believe what she had just seen. It was hard to believe that her best friend had just been murdered by a man called Tom Edison. His name reminded her of Thomas Edison who she had learnt about in History. "Why did Tom Edison have murder weapons? How did he know that we were in his lair?" Jayden pondered. The questions were endless. As soon as her mum's car stopped outside their house, Jayden leaped out of the car and dashed to her room. Jayden's walls were a light blue and her floor was covered in a thick woolly carpet. She had a wooden white desk in the corner of her room where her laptop was kept. By her bed there was a night stand with a lamp on it. The curtains were made of translucent fabric, and there was a wardrobe by the entrance to her room. Inside the wardrobe was Jayden's school uniform and her clothes. Her shoes were in a drawer below the wardrobe. There was a sturdy hook on her door where her heavy schoolbag and P.E kit was kept. Hurriedly, Jayden yanked her laptop out of her desk and started typing. There was only one person who would know what to do, and if he did not know what to do, all hope was lost. "Finally! I've found Detective James Wood's number, " Jayden almost shouted. "Now, to phone him." The call to James Wood was successful but painfully slow (it took five times for him to answer). "Hello, is this James Wood?" "Presently speaking." "My name is Jayden and my friend has been murdered by a scientist called Tom Edison." "A murder! Don't worry, I will arrest the person who committed such a crime. Now, give me details." After that, James Wood hung up. For the first time since the murder she finally realized the severity of what had happened.

Chapter 18

"Hello? Is anyone home? Shannon?" "The door is unlocked Jayden, you can come in." Jayden nervously entered Shannon's now lonely house. Ever since Jackson died it had been lonely, and an unhappy place for Jayden. "Shannon, I've brought the medicine with me." "Ok, let's get this over and done with." Jayden took a glass out of the cabinet and poured some water into it. After that, she produced some strange pills out of her pocket. "Shannon, would you like the pills in the water or would you like to have them separately?" "Please leave them on the side." "Yeah, no problem. Hey good luck. I hope it works, for Izzy's sake she can't lose you too." "Thanks, it will work. I will go to the doctor tomorrow and make sure. I will never leave my baby. I will fight this with all I have got." And with that Jayden was gone. Shannon picked up the glass off the counter and drank it in one go, and swallowed the pills. That night she hoped and prayed that it would work, and hat the doctors would give her the all clear. Her son died for it, for goodness' sake! She had just taken the pills that Jayden had stolen off the scientist and hoped it worked. The next day Shannon went to the doctors she was very nervous and shy and they ran test after test after test, but they couldn't find anything. They were all confused. Shannon didn't care, she was clear and could say that her son had died for a good cause. He was a hero. SHE WAS CURED!!!

Chapter 19

James investigated the case in Island Health Hospital. He strolled in slowly and glared at everyone in the room until they went quiet. As he walked to reception, he laid an eye on Agnes. She looked away. The detective was making everyone feel intimidated, as he asked with a tough voice: "Excuse me but where is Ms Johnson?" The receptionist answered uncomfortably, "She is over there, " and pointed. He stealthily walked towards where Zo was. This only took him a few of seconds, and when he reached it he stopped. Zo looked very surprised to see him there, especially as she didn't know why he was here. "I have heard about an incident involving you that happened here." he explained slowly, trying to make Zo intimidated. He asked again in a deeper voice, even slower. "Did an incident involving you happen here?" "No. I don't know where you got that information, but it is false. Nothing has happened. Now I will be off. You need to stop wasting my time." As she was walking off the detective (James) grabbed her by the arm. "I know something happened between you and Agnes." He whispered. "I also know that you are lying to save her. That is a criminal offense. You could go to jail for lying to a police officer. I will let you off this time, but you will have to sort it out by yourself." "I-I-I-I swear nothing happened!" "If you say so" The detective slowly walked along the long corridors and out of the entrance. Zo turned to where Agnes was standing but she had gone. Zo didn't know whether that was a good idea to cover for her, but it was too late now. The detective and Agnes where gone, out of her life and she could just get on with it. Now, she needed to get on with the job she loved surrounded by the people she loved.

Chapter 20

"Ahhhhh! I can't believe hasn't even finished my time machine yet! He's only finished the cure for cancer and now he's gone and had it stolen from him! Oh my gosh, I am so angry with him. Why did I hire him in the first place?" She got in her car and told her driver to drive to the Canary Wharf prison. He did so, but whilst they were in the car Bella Tron remembered she had a stash of sweets in the bottom pocket, so she ate them. This put her in a good mood, but she would be angry, very angry as she would have to spend a lot of money on this annoying scientist.

"Thank you, thank you, thank you!" The scientist said. "You will fix my time machine first, ok?" "Yes, yes, of course!" "Good. Now you will have 24 hours ok and by then it has to be finished. Yes?" "Yes, yes, of course that's all I need." They headed back to the not-so-secret lair in complete silence. The scientist was fearful for his life as he knew what Bella Tron was capable of, and he knew she wasn't afraid to do it A few days left, Bella Tron met up with the scientist: "I did it! I finished the time machine!" "Good! Now I have a special treat for you." She said in a menacing way. Bella Tron pulled out a gun and pointed it at the scientist. One shot fired and the scientist fell to the floor. Dead. She took his body out to the back yard and dug a hole. She then dumped his body covered it up with fresh soil. She had everything: POWER, a time machine, the cure for cancer to save her parents. This was all she needed to continue in life. "Although I do need another scientist, maybe that family could come in some use" mumbled Bella Tron, followed by an evil laugh. She had made a plan to become closer friends with Shannon and then offer her a job. "That's a win-win situation, she gets money for house improvements and I get more minions, I mean scientists, I mean friends. Maybe they will fall for my traps and they are soon to be my slaves, muhahahahaaaaaaaaa."

Chapter 21

Jayden went to The Edward's house. When Jayden arrived Jayden and Jackson talked about school and just life in general, but after a long conversation about school Jayden decided to ask Jackson about what has been going on lately. "Jackson, can I ask you something?" Jayden said suddenly. "Sure, you can ask me anything, " Jackson answered. "Why have you been acting so strangely lately?" Jayden asked nervously.

"Oh, well, actually there is something going on. It's my mum, she's sick really sick She has cancer." Jackson said with a tear falling from his face. "Oh, I didn't know I am so sorry." Jayden said, comforting Jackson. Jayden had to go home after that. Later that day, Jackson arrived at the counselling session. He was fifteen minutes early and looked like he had been crying a lot his eyes were bloodshot. He sat down on the lime-green sofa for a few minutes. He was very quiet and introverted. He looked like he was in deep thought so Zo did not want to disturb him, yet she knew something was not right so she urged herself to. She asked him if he wanted some biscuits or a drink. He refused the offer of biscuits but he asked for a glass of water, although he only took a sip. He was a young boy of fifteen and he had a lot of responsibility to deal with. He would normally be at home doing chores instead of going out with his friends. He was as responsible as a young teenager and he would grow into a respectful gentlemen. Zo took Jackson into a more private room and shut the doors. She waited for Jackson to start talking and open up about his feelings but he stayed quiet and reserved. Zo waited a little bit longer but there was still an awkward silence.

"So how are you today?" "I'm alright, I guess." mumbled Jackson "Are you sure?" Asked Zo in a worried and sad tone. "Well, my mum does have cancer! How am I supposed to feel!?" said Jackson raising his voice in a harsh tone. Zo tried to handle this in a very professional way. "I understand that but there's no need to shout. It's OK, I'm going to help you."

Sniffling and crying he asks, "But it's not OK is it? You haven't got a cure for cancer have you? No! I didn't think so and it's not your mum who has cancer it's my mum, my mum who is slowly dying of cancer and there's nothing I can do to help her! You don't know how helpless I feel!" "Actually, I do know how you feel. I went through the same thing my husband died from cancer and he didn't tell me he had it until he was taking his last breath on his deathbed. So yes, I do know how it feels to have someone close to you who has cancer." Zo said remembering her past. "Umm sorry about that I'm just really emotional right now because I only found out today an-." He was interrupted by Zo. "It's OK. There's no need to apologize. I understand." "Also, sorry. I know we are running out of time, but I know my mum hasn't told my little sister that she has cancer and I don't know what to do. Can you please give me some advice?" "Sure. I think that you should speak to your mum because she might have a plan about how or when she wants to tell your sister. Is that all you want to talk to me about?" "No, one last thing would it be possible for my sister, Izzy, to have some counselling sessions too?" "Definitely, but she would have to do a trial session just like you did today. Are you OK now?" asked Zo, concerned. "Yeah... I'm fine, I guess." "Are you sure?" "No, I'm not really sure. How are people supposed feel in these type of situations?" "Alright sit down" said Zo sadly. "I-I-I don't know what to do. I can't help her. I am powerless, knowing she is slowly dying. I still have to be a good son and a big brother to my sister, who does not know anything. I feel like I'm wearing a mask when I'm around them." Zo knew exactly how he felt. She had experienced the same thing. She knew all of the pain he was going through and all the pain that was to come. After calming down, Jackson got ready to leave. Jackson slowly picked up his coat and headed towards the door. He took one last look towards Zo and she was staring at him. She looked sad, like there was something she wasn't telling him. "Thank you. I really appreciate it. I feel like you're the only person I can talk to about this whole situation." And with that Jackson was gone.

Once Jackson had headed out of the door Zo put her head in her hands. Her thoughts were telling her to go after him, try and get him some help. However, her body didn't want to move. The amount that Jackson had to deal with made Zo's memories come back to haunt her. Jackson was walking down the corridor with a feeling of guilt in his stomach. He felt like some of the things he said, he shouldn't have said. Anyway, his mum had the worst of it. She had cancer after all. She had to deal with him, his sister, and the doctors. The cancer. Jackson thought to himself that he was not going to moan about anything more after that. His life was easy compared to some, including his mum's.

Chapter 22

Izzy walked towards shut door. She could hear her mum talking. Izzy knocked on the door and slowly peeked her head through. Her mum, who was staring out of the window, didn't react. Izzy walked to the window seat and sat next to her mum. She asked her if she was alright. There was no response. The little girl felt disowned by her mother. Her mums face was pale like a piece of blank paper. Tear rolled down her cheeks. "Mum, do you have cancer?" she mumbled. "Yes" This was a sad moment for both of them but Shannon felt good that she told her. She didn't have to keep lying. Shannon's eyes started to well up. She couldn't express her embarrassment and guilt. She looked at Izzy. "I'm so sorry Izzy that I kept all this from you. I thought you wouldn't understand. You are only thirteen. I feel so guilty. I'm really sorry. Please accept my apology, " wept Shannon.

Chapter 23

"Jackson, come to the living room please, " Shannon shouted. "OK Mum!" Jackson yelled back. Jackson made his way to the living room and sat on the couch opposite his mum. "Jackson, remember when I told you about my cancer?" Shannon asked. "Yes, " Jackson mumbled sorrowfully "Well, it's gotten worse but I'm getting some treatment." "Mum, you do know that they can't cure your cancer with that treatment if it's worse, right?" "I know, but we can't just give up hope. I can't just give up my life, my family, my hope, " Shannon said, tears filling up her eyes like a well filling up with water. "But there's no point!" Jackson yelled, his eyes also full of tears. "There's nothing we can do about your cancer if it's in a later stage and you know that, " Jackson continued, "so why do it, why treat the untreatable? It makes no sense to me." "Jackson, look at it from my point of view-" "No! You're desperate, so you're not thinking straight!" Jackson stormed out of the living room, tears clouding his vision, and the sound of his mum weeping echoed in his mind. He dragged himself to his room to cry like he had before. While Jackson had tears spilling out of his eyes, down his face. His mum came into his room to comfort him. "Don't worry, it's all right, " she said. "But it's not alright, it's not all right! We're keeping too many secrets!" At eight o' clock Jackson went to bed and fell straight asleep after a tiring day. He had a dream about his mum, the sound of her crying, weeping echoed in his mind and he saw a her crying tears of blood as she was slowly dying.

Chapter 24

As Shannon got on the 277 to the hospital, she felt anxious. She had so many questions that might not have any answers. What would happen to her kids? Would they have to go into care? Who would have them during treatment? All these thoughts where running around her mind at the same time. She would have to push these questions out of her mind for now. Otherwise she might not have another chance.

The bus ride felt longer than usual. She was still thinking of the questions when she booked in. This made the man at reception very annoyed because she wasn't making any sense. It took ten minutes for the lady on the desk to work out who her appointment was with. She only snapped back to planet Earth when her name was called. Shannon's steps where a lot quicker this time. She wanted to use up all her time wisely. She had so many questions and only an hour to ask them all. As soon as Agnus sat down, Shannon began asking all her questions. "Where will my kids go? Will I lose my hair? How will this..." But before she could finish Agnus stood up and touched her shoulder softly. This made Shannon calm and slow down. "Right, start again and take your time."

So Shannon started it all again, but this time slower and calmer. Agnus answered all the questions she medically knew the answers to. "So, how do you feel about all this?" Agnus asked generally concerned. "I know you are worried about your kids, but you have to look after yourself first. If you can't look after yourself, how are you meant to look after your children as well?" Shannon just stared at her like she had just said the smartest thing in the world. How was she meant to help her children when she can't even help herself? Everything made sense to her from that moment onwards. They both spent the next 20 minutes talking about their lives. Agnus gave advice to Shannon and Shannon gave advice to Agnus. The hour seemed to last forever and Shannon began to wonder why she had been fretting on the bus so much. Agnus gave Shannon some numbers to call if she ever got stuck with the kids, and some of her treatment plans. She was given two options by Agnus: chemotherapy or radiotherapy. As soon as she said this it hit Shannon on the head: this is really real. The biggest question that Shannon had was what she could do with her children during treatment. She had no family around her and they were too young (in her mind) to look after themselves. "Do you have any neighbours you are friendly with around here" Agnus asked politely. "There is Lola around the corner. She's brilliant with the kids and is always very happy to help but she's not always available" She didn't have any more questions, but there was still 35 minutes left. They sat in silence for the next five minutes, until Agnus said, "I know how you feel, you know - no-one to talk to, and you don't think anyone understands what you are going through. Well I do. Even though it might be a little different, I feel the same. Remember you always regret what you never did in life." Shannon didn't know what she meant by this, but she knew it would have some relevance in her life sooner or later. Maybe this meant she didn't have much time left, or maybe no one knew if the treatment would work. All she knew was she needed to get back to her children. There were still 15 minutes of the session left. "Have you ever thought about putting your children into care homes?" Shannon didn't even know how to respond to this. Her face turned bright red and she yelled at Agnus, "I would never abandon my children, no matter how bad it gets!" Agnus was taken aback by the sudden anger. "I only meant it as a suggestion. I am really sorry if I have made you angry." "Why did this have to happen to me? I have done nothing to deserve this!" Shannon started to cry uncontrollably. Agnus didn't know what to do. She just stood and stared. Shannon didn't stop, but Agnus couldn't take it. She ran out of the room and left Shannon by herself in a state of despair. She couldn't take it anymore. Shannon sat there crying until the session was over. She then staggered, with all her make-up smudged, to the bus stop and took the bus home. Agnus returned to find Shannon gone. She went to go and get a doctor as she didn't know what to do in these situations. When she found Shannon gone she suddenly went to the front desk to try and phone her. When there was no answer, Agnus got really worried but Shannon had booked another appointment on the way out. Agnus was glad she would see her soon.

Chapter 25

Agnus woke up at 7 o'clock in the morning and remembered that she had her counselling session that day. She quickly got out of bed and went straight to her wardrobe to pick out her outfit, which took her a while to do because she was very indecisive. She had a bath for 10 minutes, ironed her clothes, washed her face and puts on her red stripped hoodie, her blue pebble-washed jeans and some white trainers. She picked up her bag and dropped her keys and her Oyster card in her black rucksack. She left the house and locked the door. She then made her way to her nearest bus stop and caught the D8 to go to Canary Wharf Therapy. She sat on the bus on the top deck, at the front when the bus jerked to a stop. Agnus dropped all of her paperwork. Once she arrived. She looked across the road. There was the counselling centre. The sight of the tall glass building sent a chill down her spine and she shivered. She was so focused on the large sky scraper that she stepped into the road without noticing. A car zoomed past her and beeped, the man in the car leaned out of the window and shouted. "Oi! Watch it, you coulda been a pancake!" "S-sorry!" Agnus apologised. "Road rage much, " she mumbled to herself. Agnus entered the tall, glass building. After booking in, she stared into space and imagined the walls closing in on her. Everyone around observed her actions and noticed that she was extremely nervous. She tried to avoid eye contacts with everyone. Agnus was soon called in to the room with Zo. She was very sacred and was very tense. She was very uncomfortable and forgot to take her medication this morning and started to go crazy. The nurse screamed for and attempted to strangle Zo. Realising what she had done, she ran out of the room. *THE END*

23264246R00074

Printed in Great Britain
by Amazon